This Book Belongs to

_____

Books for Kids: Big Ideas for Bright Minds

All About Barbie

by Shirley Bell

ISBN: 9798854291934

Children Non-Fiction - Barbie Doll - Toys - History - Biography

All About Barbie

Chapter 1
The Magic of Barbie

"Love and imagination
can change the world."
— Barbie as Rapunzel, 2002

Before smartphones, before video games, and even before the internet, there was a doll. But she wasn't just any doll. She was Barbie. To understand why Barbie is so special, imagine a time when every toy had a set story. A teddy bear was just a cuddly friend. A toy soldier had its battles. But Barbie? Barbie was a blank canvas, a world of possibilities.

Many dolls before Barbie were like babies. You could pretend to be their parent, feed them, and put them to bed. That was sweet, of course. But Barbie was different. With her, you could dream of the future. You could imagine being a fashion designer today, an astronaut tomorrow, and a race car driver the day after.

Why is Barbie so important? Because she wasn't just a toy. For many, she was a glimpse into the future, a promise of what could be. She represented freedom, choice, and endless possibility. In a time when many girls were told to dream within limits, Barbie whispered, *"Dream big. Be anything."*

Barbie broke the mold of what a doll could be. She came into the world when women were starting to demand more rights, more respect, and more opportunities. Barbie was not just a reflection of the times but also a hopeful glimpse into a future full of possibilities. She was an icon in every sense.

Dolls Before Barbie

For as long as humans have told stories, they have also played with dolls. From ancient civilizations using clay, wood, or bone, to the porcelain dolls of the 19th century, dolls have always held a special place in our hearts. They were not just playthings but also treasured possessions, often passed down from one generation to the next.

In ancient Egypt, dolls were made with painted clay and adorned with bits of cloth or yarn. The ancient Greeks had jointed dolls made of clay or wood. Children in ancient Rome played with dolls made of wax or terracotta. Throughout history, dolls were not just toys but also a reflection of society, culture, and the times.

By the 20th century, dolls had become a big business. The Industrial Revolution brought about new materials like celluloid and, later on, plastic. This meant that for the first time in history dolls could be produced faster, in bigger numbers, and more affordable.

The story of Barbie begins in 1950s America. After the devastation of World War II, this was a time when there was a strong desire to return to normalcy, to rebuild, and to look forward to a brighter future. Families grew, economies boomed, and the suburbs expanded.

Dolls of the post-WWII era largely mirrored traditional roles. Many dolls available to little girls were "baby dolls", emphasizing caregiving and motherhood. They were soft, cuddly, and designed for nurturing. Girls could pretend to be moms, feeding, bathing, and tucking these baby dolls into bed.

However, as the 1950s progressed, there was a sense of change in the air. Women, who had taken on various roles during the war, were now beginning to envision a world with more possibilities for themselves and their daughters. They didn't just see themselves as caregivers but also as professionals, dreamers, and achievers.

And it was against this backdrop that the idea of Barbie, a grown-up, fashion-forward doll, was born. While other dolls said, *"Take care of me,"* Barbie seemed to say, *"What adventure shall we have today?"*

Did you know?

In the 18th and 19th centuries, dolls that resembled "little women" were quite common, but they were not meant for children. These intricately crafted dolls were referred to as "fashion dolls," and they were famous with collectors. They were also used in fashion shops, as a kind of catalog.

These dolls featured porcelain faces that were hand-painted, articulated bodies, and elaborate wigs made of human hair. But it was their wardrobe that was truly stunning. Their miniature dresses captured every little detail of the latest fashion, down to the petticoat and stockings.

In the 1860s, a new technique called bisque allowed doll-makers to use molds to mass-produce these sought-after dolls. By the end of the 19th century, shops all over Europe featured fashion dolls as tridimensional, interactive displays. Companies like Jumeau, Kestner, and Simon & Halbig became prominent manufacturers of bisque dolls during this time.

Even Thomas Edison joined in the fade when he designed his "Singing Doll" in 1890. She featured the usual articulated body and bisque porcelain face, but her chest was made out of a metal box. Inside the metal chest, there were wax audio cylinders that were used to generate a playback of nursery rhymes. Unfortunately, the technology of the time was not quite there yet and Edison's Singing Doll broke easily. It would still be a few decades before singing dolls would become a commercial hit.

Barbie has inspired generations of young girls worldwide, allowing them to dream of worlds where anything is possible. Today, the moment when a young girl receives her first Barbie doll has become almost a rite of passage, a sign that she's no longer a "little kid," but is moving on to the age when one starts to dream about *what will I be when I grow up?*

What about you? Which was your first Barbie doll? Who gave it to you? Was it a heirloom, a doll that once belonged to your mom or older sister? Or maybe you're still dreaming of your first Barbie? Which is your favorite "Barbie" and why? As we embark on this adventure, take a moment to reflect on what Barbie means to you.

Barbie and Me

My first Barbie was _____.

I was _____ years old when I got my first Barbie, and it was given to me by_____ as a

_____ gift.

My favorite Barbie is _____

because _____

_____.

I wish that I had the following Barbie and accessories _____

_____.

because _____

_____.

_____

What I like the most about Barbie is _____

_____

_____

_____

_____

Chapter 2
The Daring Creator

"Barbie always represented the fact
that a woman has choices."

- Ruth Handler

Every hero, real or fictional, has an origin story. And for Barbie, that story starts with a visionary woman named Ruth Handler. If Barbie were to call someone "Mom," it would be Ruth. Why? Because Ruth is the brilliant mind behind Barbie's creation. Just as authors give life to characters in books, Ruth breathed life into Barbie, turning a simple idea into a doll that would capture the imaginations of millions worldwide. Let's journey into the life of Ruth Handler and uncover how she dreamt up Barbie, the world's most famous doll.

Ruth Handler: Background and Early Life

Ruth Mosko was born in Denver, Colorado, in 1916, to Polish-Jewish immigrant parents. Growing up in a modest household, Ruth learned early on the importance of hard work and perseverance. She was bright, ambitious, and always had an eye for opportunity. In her teenage years, Ruth met her future husband, Elliot Handler, and the two shared an undeniable bond and a passion for design and creativity.

Even as a young woman, Ruth's sense of style and creativity shone brightly. Growing up, she displayed an interest in crafting and often experimented with fabrics, sometimes making her own clothes or redesigning old ones. Friends and family would often find her engrossed in sketching designs or sewing, turning a simple piece of cloth into a stylish outfit.

While Ruth didn't have formal training in design, she possessed a natural flair for it. Her friends often commented on how she had a keen eye for detail and an uncanny ability to predict fashion trends. This self-taught talent would later play a crucial role in Barbie's fashionable wardrobe.

When Ruth met Elliot, it was like two pieces of a puzzle fitting perfectly together. Elliot, an artist at heart, was studying industrial design. He would often craft small art pieces and toys from wood, and Ruth, with her love for textiles, would sometimes add fabric elements to them. Their early projects showcased a blend of Elliot's functional design principles and Ruth's aesthetic touches.

They would spend hours brainstorming ideas, drawing sketches, and bringing them to life. Their mutual love for creating wasn't just a shared interest; it was a bond that drew them closer together. Whether it was collaborating on a new toy concept or Ruth trying out a new dress design with Elliot's feedback, their partnership was a fusion of two creative minds feeding off each other's energy.

Once Upon a Toy: The Origins of Mattel

The Handlers married in 1938 when they were both 22 years old. The couple then moved to Los Angeles, where they started their family - and what would become one of the world's greatest toy empires: Mattel.

The story of Mattel, one of the world's most renowned toy companies, began not with grand ambitions, but with a simple partnership and a shared dream. Founded in 1945 by Ruth and Elliot Handler, along with a third partner, Harold "Matt" Matson, Mattel's name cleverly combines parts of "Matt" and "Elliot." It's a testament to the collaboration and unity that birthed the brand.

Launching a business post-World War II was no easy feat. Resources were scarce, and the Handlers invested their savings to kickstart their vision. Initially, Mattel started not as a toy manufacturer but as a picture frame company. The company crafted beautiful frames, with Elliot designing and overseeing the production and Ruth managing the business side. They worked out of a garage, symbolizing the quintessential American start-up story.

But it wasn't long before their ingenuity led them down a different path. Using the scrap material left over from the frame production, they began crafting dollhouse furniture. It was a hit! The shift from frames to toys was a natural progression, driven by demand and the Handlers' keen sense for market needs. As the years went by, Mattel's toy range expanded, but the core principle remained the same: to produce innovative and entertaining toys that children loved.

In the company's early years, Elliot's role was primarily in design and product development. His creativity and eye for detail gave Mattel's toys a unique edge. Ruth, on the other hand, was the driving force behind the scenes. Her keen business acumen helped navigate the company through its initial challenges, and she played a pivotal role in marketing and business strategy.

The Spark of an Idea

While they were busy fulfilling children's dreams, the Handlers were tending to their own family as well. Their daughter Barbara was born in 1944 and in 1947 they welcomed their son Kenneth. The Handlers' home was filled with laughter, love, and play. The children were called Barbie and Ken by their loving parents, names that would soon be as familiar to generations of children as "Santa Claus."

Ruth, ever the observant mother, took a special interest in her children's playtime. She noticed an intriguing pattern: while Barbara and her friends enjoyed playing mommy with their baby dolls, by the time they were six, the girls started to become more interested in paper cut-out dolls.

These weren't just any dolls. These cut-outs, shaped like little women, were gateways to the girls' dreams. Through them, the girls would step into the world of adulthood, trying on roles of powerful businesswomen one day and glamorous movie stars the next. They played out stories of independence, ambition, and exciting adventures.

This realization kindled a question in Ruth's heart: What if there was a doll—a real, tangible doll—that could become anything a girl envisioned? A toy that wasn't limited to the role of a baby, but rather mirrored the endless possibilities of the future.

13

The universe, it seemed, was listening to Ruth's musings. During a family trip to Europe in 1956, in a quaint toy store in Germany, Ruth's eyes landed on something familiar yet foreign - a doll named Bild Lilli. With her fashionable outfits and adult-like figure, Bild Lilli was the embodiment of Ruth's idea. Ironically, Lilli wasn't designed for children at all. She was based on a cheeky German comic strip character and was mostly bought as a novelty gift for adults.

But where others saw a trinket, Ruth saw potential. She purchased several Bild Lilli dolls, thinking of them not just as souvenirs but as muses for her grand vision. These dolls, with their unique style and grown-up appeal, solidified Ruth's conviction. She wasn't merely inspired; she was determined to bring to American children a doll that would empower them to dream boundlessly. This trip, and the discovery of Lilli, set the stage for the birth of Barbie.

Did you know?

Cut-out dolls have a rich history in Asia, and are associated with shadow puppet theater. This is a form of entertainment that dates back to millennia, and can still be found in traditional festivals in China and Japan today.

The setup is quite simple, but the results are amazing! A light source, traditionally a candle or oil lamp, is placed behind a translucent screen. The cut-out dolls are then placed between the light and the screen. Manipulated by skilled puppeteers using thin rods, the dolls come alive, their shadows magnified, bringing the storytelling to live. As the light flickers, it lends the characters an ethereal, almost magical quality, making the narratives they portray even more enchanting.

And the best about shadow theater is that it's so simple you can do it yourself. All you need is:

Shadow screen: a sheet of tracing or baking paper attached to a frame.

Light source: a flashlight or a spotlight lamp placed behind the shadow screen at a safe distance (too close and you might set the paper on fire!)

Cutout dolls: stiff paper like cardboard boxes for the cutouts, pencils for sketching the designs, and scissors for cutting them. To manipulate the cutouts, glue barbecue skewers.

And of course, a lot of creativity!

The secret to a good cutout doll for a shadow theater is a strong silhouette. On the next page there are some designs you can copy to get you started. Good luck, have fun, and be careful with those scissors.

Please inform a supervising adult before you start, explaining the steps involved with the cutouts and the setup of the theater to make sure you don't injure yourself or others.

Chapter 3
Designing Barbie

"The most beautiful thing
you can be is yourself."

Barbie: Mariposa, 2008

Ruth Handler returned home bringing a suitcase full of Bild Lilli dolls, and bursting with ideas. The Bild Lilli gave Ruth the confirmation that she was on the right track, that her novel proposal of a grown-up doll was not as far-fetched as the toy industry would have her think. But while Lilli was unique and eye-catching, she wasn't quite the doll Ruth had dreamt of.

Bild Lilli's grown-up look was a bit too serious for the young girls Ruth was thinking of. Lilli had been designed as a playful wink for adults, but Ruth's vision was different. She wanted a doll that girls could see as an older sister, a guide into the world of grown-ups.

But what to call this new doll? Inspiration struck close to home. Ruth had been inspired by watching her own daughter play, so naming the doll "Barbie" after Barbara was like adding the cherry on top of a sundae. It was a perfect blend of inspiration and affection.

In her mind's eye, Ruth imagined a doll that was a mix of Hollywood glam, trendy fashion, and the adventurous spirit she saw in her daughter, Barbara, and her friends. And Ruth was in the right place to soak in all the inspiration Hollywood had to offer! When the Handlers first moved to Los Angeles, before starting their own company together, Ruth had worked at Paramount movie studios. And the allure of the glamorous movie stars stuck with her.

And Ruth wasn't alone. In the mid-1950s, Hollywood wasn't just a place; it was a dream. The movie industry was in its golden age, and cinemas were like gateways to enchanted worlds. When the lights dimmed, and the screen lit up, audiences were transported to places they could only dream of, and at the heart of these dreams were the stars.

Names like Marilyn Monroe, Audrey Hepburn, and Elizabeth Taylor weren't just actresses—they were icons. Marilyn, with her platinum blond hair and infectious smile, personified glamour. Audrey Hepburn, in her iconic little black dress in "Breakfast at Tiffany's", defined elegance. And Elizabeth Taylor, with her dazzling violet eyes, was the epitome of Hollywood beauty.

Young girls looked up to these stars, not just for their acting, but also for their style. Every movie premiere or awards show was an opportunity to see the latest fashion trends. The dresses, the shoes, the jewelry—it was all part of the magic. These stars set the standards for beauty and grace.

19

It was more than just about clothes; it was about aspiration. Watching these actresses, young girls could imagine a world of possibilities. They could dream of being confident like Marilyn, elegant like Audrey, or as captivating as Elizabeth.

And it was this sense of glamor and aspiration that Ruth Handler tapped into when creating Barbie. The iconic curves and timeless allure of Barbie's design are a reflection of the age in which this magic doll was born. Ruth wanted to design a doll that would capture the appeal, confidence, and infinite possibilities of the movie stars that inspired her.

Barbie wasn't just a toy; she was a canvas upon which girls could paint their dreams, influenced by the allure of 1950s Hollywood.

Yet, while Ruth was the dreamer, the task of sketching and designing was better suited for someone else: Elliot, her husband. Together, they made a formidable team, with Ruth painting the dream in words and Elliot bringing it to life on paper. It was a dance of imagination and creativity, with each move meticulously planned.

And so, through strokes of creativity, collaboration, and love, Barbie was born. Not just as a doll, but as a beacon of dreams, aspirations, and endless stories waiting to be told.

Choosing the Material:
Breaking with Tradition

The 1950s were a time of change and innovation. The world was emerging from the shadows of a great war, and people were eager to embrace the future. One of the most exciting signs of this new age was a versatile and shiny material called plastic.

Plastic was suddenly everywhere. Imagine a world where almost overnight, everyday items began to transform. Shoes that used to be made of leather now had shiny plastic heels. Handbags that were once only woven or leather were now available in bright and colorful plastics. Clothes had plastic buttons, and kitchens were adorned with plastic handles, gadgets, and more. This material wasn't just popular—it was revolutionary!

Against this backdrop, Mattel, founded by Ruth and Elliot, initially crafted toys out of wood, reflecting the traditions of toy-making. Wood was familiar, warm, and had a timeless quality. But as the world around them changed, so did their vision.

Ruth and Elliot realized something crucial: if Barbie was going to be the dream doll they imagined, she couldn't be made of wood. She needed to have smooth skin, bendable limbs, and be able to be produced on a large scale to reach every little girl who dreamt of her. Plastic was the answer.

This new, modern material was not only durable but also allowed for intricate designs. With the latest molding technologies, creating a doll like Barbie with detailed features became a reality.

And so, in a world where everything from fashion to household items was being transformed by the magic of plastic, Barbie too began her journey, embracing the spirit of modernity and innovation.

Convincing Mattel: The Dream vs. The Doubts

In the late 1950s, Mattel was growing, but it wasn't the toy titan it would become. The company was still finding its footing in the toy industry, primarily known for its musical toys, board games, and of course, wooden toys. Nestled in its headquarters, a modest but bustling space filled with designers, marketers, and toy enthusiasts, Mattel was always on the lookout for the next big thing.

But when Ruth Handler brought forward the concept of Barbie, it wasn't met with the enthusiasm she had hoped for. The toy industry, like any other, had its traditions. And one of those long-standing traditions was the kind of dolls that were produced: cute, cuddly baby dolls. These dolls were cherished because they allowed girls to emulate being caregivers, mirroring the nurturing roles they often saw their mothers play.

Barbie was different. With her adult-like figure, chic fashion sense, and confident demeanor, she was more than just a doll; she was a statement. To many at Mattel, this statement was too loud, too bold. There were whispers around the office. Would parents buy such a doll for their daughters? Could it possibly compete with the beloved baby dolls?

Ruth, however, saw what others didn't. She wasn't just pitching a doll; she was presenting a vision. Ruth spoke about the changing times, about the new Hollywood-inspired dreams girls had, and about the aspirational play that Barbie could offer.

But perhaps the most significant hurdle wasn't just explaining her idea—it was battling doubt. Some thought Barbie might be a passing fad or too niche. Others were concerned about the production costs of such a detailed doll, especially in material as novel as plastic.

Yet, with every objection, Ruth had a counter. She explained the gap in the market, showcased preliminary sketches and even shared anecdotes of her own daughter's play habits. She believed in Barbie's potential, not just as a toy but as a movement. And slowly but surely, she began to turn the tide of opinion within Mattel.

Prototyping in the 1950s

Bringing Barbie to life was an intricate ballet of design, engineering, and trial and error. In the late 1950s, while plastic had become increasingly popular, using it to create a detailed, durable, and mass-producible doll was a significant challenge. The world of toy manufacturing was entering new territory, and Mattel was at its forefront.

Initially, several prototypes were made, each trying to refine and perfect Barbie's design. Estimates suggest that close to a dozen prototypes were developed, each one bringing them closer to the final product. While Mattel had its own manufacturing facilities, the complexity of Barbie, especially her mold, required expertise that wasn't readily available in-house. As a result, Mattel collaborated with specialized external companies that had experience in detailed plastic molding.

The person credited with designing the first Barbie mold was Jack Ryan, a talented engineer at Mattel. Jack, along with his team, faced numerous challenges. The molding process began with a sculptor crafting a clay model of Barbie, much larger than the doll's intended size. This oversized model allowed for meticulous detailing. Once the clay model was approved, it was used to create a metal mold, which was then shrunk down to Barbie's actual size, ensuring every detail was captured.

Creating the mold was one thing, but producing a doll that could withstand play was another. The first prototypes had paint that chipped too easily, hair that wasn't quite right, and limbs that were too stiff or too loose. The paint had to be reformulated multiple times to find the right balance between durability and appearance. Meanwhile, the hunt for the perfect doll hair led them to a synthetic material that could be styled, brushed, and even washed without losing its luster.

One of the primary concerns was Barbie's limbs. Ruth wanted a doll with posable limbs, but the joints had to be both smooth-moving and robust. This required several revisions to get right. The team also worked diligently to ensure that the plastic didn't have any sharp edges or points, prioritizing the safety of the children who'd play with Barbie.

The journey from an idea to a tangible, playable Barbie was filled with countless hours of design, testing, and refinement. But every challenge overcome, every hurdle crossed, brought them one step closer to introducing a doll that would change the toy industry forever.

The Ultimate Test: Playtime with Real Kids

Even with the internal battles at Mattel and the challenges of prototyping, there was one test that would prove to be the most crucial of all: how would real kids react to Barbie?

Ruth, always having her daughter Barbara in mind when conceptualizing the doll, knew exactly where to start. One sunny afternoon, in the backyard of the Handler residence, a special play session was organized. A small group of Barbara's friends—about eight girls in total—were invited over for what they thought was just another day of play. Little did they know, they were about to become some of the first children in the world to lay their hands on a Barbie prototype.

Tables were set with a variety of Barbie dolls, each slightly different from the other, sporting different outfits, hairstyles, and accessories. Ruth, trying to be as discreet as possible, observed from a distance, her heart racing. She watched as the girls' eyes widened, their faces lit up, and an audible gasp filled the air. They were drawn to Barbie dolls like magnets.

As the afternoon progressed, Ruth took notes. Which outfits did they prefer? Did they enjoy styling Barbie's hair? Were the movable limbs a hit or a miss? But more than the specifics, she was looking for that magical spark — the gleam in a child's eye when they connect with a toy.

The feedback was overwhelmingly positive. The girls loved Barbie's adult-like figure, imagining all sorts of scenarios from glamorous Hollywood premieres to adventurous travels around the world. They styled her hair, changed her outfits multiple times, and even introduced Barbie to their other toys. It was a world of imaginative play, and Barbie was at its center.

Ruth listened intently as the girls shared their likes and dislikes, their wishes and desires for the doll. It was this invaluable feedback that allowed for refinements before Barbie's official launch.

Did you know?

Trendy hairstyles would become Barbie's hallmark of Barbie, always keeping up with the latest fashion and celebrity styles.

Can you name these popular hairdos? Solution on the next page.

1 Afro
2 Beehive
3 Blunt bob
4 Braided bun
5 Cornrow
6 Curly bob
7 Emo
8 Feathered long
9 Long and sleek
10 Pixie
11 Senegalese twist
12 Shaggy bob

Solution

Long and sleek

Feathered long

Cornrow

Senegalese twist

Emo

Beehive

Braided bun

Afro

Pixie

Shaggy bob

Blunt bob

Curly bob

Chapter 4
A Star is Born

"The power to change the world
has been inside you all along."

— Barbie in Princess Power, 2015

It took three years from Ruth's original idea about a new revolutionary doll to the day that the first Barbie was ready for the world. And true to style, Barbie's debut was nothing short of spectacular. Just like the Hollywood stars that inspired Ruth's vision, Barbie made her entrance on the red carpet — red carpet for toys, that was.

For Barbie and Mattel, this event that would change the history of the company and of toys forever was the *American International Toy Fair of 1959*. It was like making a debut at the biggest blockbuster movie of the year.

The Road to the Toy Fair: Anticipation and Preparation

The weeks leading up to the Toy Fair were a whirlwind of activity at Mattel's headquarters. Stacks of design sketches, color swatches, and packaging prototypes covered the tables. The air was thick with a mix of excitement and tension.

Ruth, as the visionary behind Barbie, was at the epicenter of it all. Meetings ran late into the night, discussing everything from Barbie's booth design at the fair to the final touches on the doll's outfit. Every detail, no matter how minute, was pored over, ensuring that Barbie would be presented in the best possible light.

Inside Mattel, the anticipation was palpable. For many, Barbie was not just another product. She represented years of hard work, creativity, and passion. She was a bold venture, stepping away from the conventional and banking on the hope that the world was ready for something new.

As the days dwindled down, the team faced the regular last-minute hitches—shipment delays, tweaks to the display booth, and rehearsing the pitch to potential retailers. Ruth, despite her confidence in Barbie, couldn't help but feel a flutter of nerves. What if the world didn't see in Barbie what she did? What if they weren't ready for this revolution in doll design?

The night before the Toy Fair, the Mattel team gathered for a final briefing. Ruth took a moment to address everyone, her voice filled with emotion. *"We've poured our hearts into this,"* she began, *"and no matter what happens tomorrow, remember that we've created something special."* The room echoed with a round of applause, not just for Barbie, but for the collective dream they were all chasing.

Barbie's World Premiere

The American International Toy Fair in New York was the grand stage for toy manufacturers, a place where dreams were built, and where trends were set for the coming year. On March 9, 1959, nestled among stalls showcasing toy trains, action figures, and plush teddy bears, was the Mattel booth – and it was about to make history.

Ruth and the Mattel team had designed a special display for Barbie. The centerpiece was a beautiful revolving pedestal showcasing the very first Barbie. Dressed in a stylish zebra-striped black-and-white swimsuit, she wore her long hair tied back in a ponytail. Her arched brows, side-glancing blue eyes, and ruby-red lips gave her a sophisticated look, a far cry from the baby dolls that dominated the scene.

Barbie was the embodiment of the dreams and the style of 1959. With her stylish hairdo and daring swimwear, featuring oversized sunglasses that were all the rage that year, she could have been on the cover of a fashion magazine. True to the business model that would come to characterize

Barbie's early years, the first Barbie was available as a blonde or as a brunette. And she came with a packed wardrobe ready to fulfill the dreams of any little girl: fancy evening gowns and stylish day dresses and accessories, hinting at the vast world of possibilities that Barbie promised.

The Toy Fair wasn't open to the public. It was an exclusive event, primarily for toy retailers, distributors, and industry insiders. So, when the curtains were drawn back to unveil Barbie, the audience was a mix of serious business folk in suits, jotting down notes, murmuring among themselves, and scrutinizing every detail.

Initial reactions were mixed. Some were immediately enchanted by

Barbie's mature design and the potential she held as a new kind of toy. Whispers of "revolutionary" and "game-changer" filled the air. Retailers from big department stores approached the booth, already envisioning the doll gracing their shelves.

However, not everyone was convinced. A few attendees raised eyebrows, questioning whether parents would buy an adult-like doll for their children. One memorable scene was of a prominent toy store owner openly expressing his doubt, only for his young daughter, who had accompanied him, to exclaim how much she loved Barbie. That moment epitomized the generational divide in the perception of Barbie.

But by the end of the fair, one thing was clear: Barbie's debut had been a splash. Orders poured in, and the Mattel team left with a sense of achievement. They had successfully introduced a star, and the world was eager to see what she would do next.

First Sales: From Showroom to Shelves

It wasn't just the press that was interested in this new adult-like doll. Toy retailers quickly saw the potential of Barbie dolls. Orders began pouring in, with stores vying to be among the first to stock Barbie on their shelves. The initial production run was modest, with Mattel hoping for steady sales. But as the dolls began appearing in store windows across America, it became evident that Barbie was in high demand.

Parents and children alike flocked to toy stores. The allure of a doll that allowed young girls to dream beyond their childhood, to envision a world of possibilities and careers, was undeniable. By the end of the year, Barbie had not just met sales expectations - she had far exceeded them.

The Barbie phenomenon wasn't contained to just the United States. News of this groundbreaking doll reached shores far and wide. From Europe to Asia, distributors sought rights to bring Barbie to their countries. Translated advertisements introduced Barbie to children across different cultures and languages, but her appeal was universal.

Word of mouth, coupled with clever marketing campaigns, propelled Barbie to iconic status in a remarkably short time. She wasn't just a doll; she was a movement, reshaping how generations of girls played and dreamt.

Did you know?

Accessorizing was always an important part of the Barbie look. From the very start, children could add a wide range of clothes, shoes and accessories to customize their Barbie to fit their style. Just like any girl, Barbie loves her collection of handbags. Can you name them all? Turn the page for the solution.

1 Baguette	5 Duffel	9 Messenger
2 Barrel	6 Frame	10 Satchel
3 Bucket	7 Hobo	11 Tote
4 Clutch	8 Kelly	12 Wristlet

What about Barbie's collection of shoes, do you know all their names?
Solution on the next page.

1. Ankle Boot
2. Ankle strap
3. Ballet flat
4. Clogs
5. Gladiator Sandals
6. Kitten heel
7. Knee boots
8. Mary Jane
9. Mule
10. Slingback
11. Stiletto
12. Wedges

Solution

Wristlet

Clutch

Barrel

Baguette

Duffel

Frame

Kelly

Messenger

Satchel

Bucket

Hobo

Tote

Stiletto

Ankle strap

Wedges

Slingback

Clogs

Mule

Kitten heel

Gladiator Sandals

Ballet flat

Mary Jane

Ankle Boot

Knee boots

Chapter 5
Barbie the Fashion Icon

"Barbie has always been an inspiration. Dressing her was part of every girl's dream."

— Reem Acra

Barbie's overnight success caught not just the world by surprise - it also meant big changes for her creators. The Mattel team, which had been a small family company until then, had to suddenly grow and expand to cope with the immense demand of the orders pouring in.

Ruth knew that fulfilling orders alone wasn't enough. Barbie was the embodiment of dreams, and dreams are alive and forever changing. If her creation was to achieve lasting success, Barbie had to keep growing and expanding. And Ruth knew exactly how. She tapped into the universal feeling of joy and delight that every little girl gets when she becomes a princess. And the trick to becoming a princess - or a doctor, or an explorer - was to have plenty of wardrobe choices.

Soon Barbie would become synonymous with fashion, being as famous for her revolutionary design as for her hundreds of outfits and accessories, plenty to fill many walk-in wardrobes not to mention the dreams of little girls worldwide.

The Magic of the Mini-Fashion World

Ruth had a vision, but she couldn't do it alone. In the vast hallways of Mattel, she brought together a team of designers, each armed with sketchbooks bursting with ideas.

"How about this?" one would ask, holding up a sketch of a mini evening gown, sparkling like the dresses Hollywood actresses wore to glamorous events. Another designer would suggest a tiny astronaut suit, reminding everyone of the women reaching for the stars. As they looked at designs, Ruth would often say, *"Remember, Barbie can be anything!"*

In the initial years under the guidance of Ruth and Eliot Handler, Barbie's wardrobe was a revolutionary game-changer. Unlike many dolls of the era who donned stiff, traditional fabrics, Barbie showcased the future. Ruth envisioned dresses for Barbie that mirrored the perfection of a full-sized grown-up outfit, right down to the tiniest button.

The team, sharing her vision, opted to utilize malleable plastics, which set Mattel's creations apart. This innovative approach meant that, unlike the rigid dresses of competing dolls, Barbie's clothes had a flexibility that allowed them to bend, twist, and fit with impeccable precision. It was as if a real ballgown had been meticulously shrunk to doll size, with every delicate fold, radiant shimmer, and dazzling sequin perfectly intact.

However, history has a way of shaping the direction of even the most iconic brands. The crude oil embargos of the 1970s and 80s dramatically impacted plastic production. The world saw shortages, which necessitated changes in production techniques and materials. This global event steered Mattel back to real fabrics for Barbie's attire. While the flexibility and durability of plastic had its advantages, the return to genuine fabrics brought with it a renewed authenticity to Barbie's wardrobe.

Today, the legacy of both the plastic and fabric eras can be seen in Barbie's outfits. Modern Barbie clothes are typically a blend of real fabrics, adorned occasionally with plastic or metallic embellishments. These outfits are not only fashion-forward but are also a testament to the brand's adaptability and commitment to mirroring real-world trends.

Advances in technology mean that even fabrics can achieve some of the malleability that plastic once offered, ensuring Barbie remains at the forefront of the miniature fashion world. And as concerns grow globally about sustainability, Mattel is also exploring eco-friendly materials and practices to ensure Barbie is not just a style icon, but also an eco-heroine.

But materials weren't the only thing the design team had to contend with. It was important that Barbie's outfits stayed current and reflected new trends and styles. Mattel's team dove deep into the fashion world. They poured over magazines, watched Hollywood films, and studied fashion shows. Hollywood stars like Audrey Hepburn, with her classic and elegant style, or the fun and funky looks of the Spice Girls, would often inspire their creations. It was important to keep up with the times and keep the dream of Barbie alive to every new generation.

However, the real thrill was when world-renowned designers came on board. Picture the Mattel design room when someone like Karl Lagerfeld walked in. The fashion legend once made Barbie a tiny version of his signature look, and the entire team was over the moon!

Yet, even as they were starstruck, they knew the real stars were the children. After all, Barbie was for them. So, they'd invite groups of eager kids to the Mattel showrooms, unveiling new outfits and watching their reactions. A gasp here, a wide-eyed wonder there; those moments told Ruth and her team they were on the right track.

Did the children have a say? Absolutely! Ruth believed that children knew best about play. So, when they said they wanted more vibrant colors or a different type of shoe, the team took notes.

In this whirlwind of sketches, fabrics, and designs, Barbie's wardrobe became an enchanting world of its own. Every dress told a story, every shoe held an adventure, and every child could create their own fairytale with Barbie leading the way.

It wasn't just about fashion; it was about dreams. And as Ruth often said, with Barbie, *"The possibilities are endless."*

Barbie's Iconic Hair: A Tress Transformation

From the moment Barbie stepped into the spotlight, her hair became a significant facet of her identity. In the beginning, Barbie's long hair was made from a material called "Saran," a soft, shiny, and long-lasting type of synthetic fiber. This gave her a natural sheen that made her stand out. As the years passed, Mattel experimented with various other synthetic materials to achieve the perfect balance of luster, playability, and style retention.

Hair is a mirror to the times, and Barbie's hairstyles evolved to reflect the prevailing trends of each era. She has spotted everything from the original "poodle" ponytail of the late 50s, to the shorter, puffy hairstyles of the 60s, to the extra long hairdos of the 70s and 90s. Today, Barbie comes in a multitude of hairstyles, even bald!

But it wasn't just about fashion; it was about innovation too. Take, for instance, the models that came with interchangeable wigs. These Barbies allowed kids to transform her look in an instant, giving them a taste of the mod trends of the 1960s. Then there were the Barbies with built-in hairstyling gimmicks. Some dolls, thanks to concealed metal wires, had hair that could be curled, straightened, and styled with just a twist of the fingers.

But Barbie wasn't the only one who underwent hair revolutions. Ken, her ever-stylish counterpart, had his moments too. Initially sporting molded hair, Ken eventually embraced real synthetic locks. But the real innovation came in the 90s with "Shaving Fun Ken." This doll had a beard that appeared with warm water and disappeared with cold, allowing kids to 'shave' him with a toy razor, truly giving a dynamic edge to playtime.

Barbie and Ken's hair became more than just an accessory. It was a canvas, a testament to changing times and technologies, and a tool that allowed kids to weave stories, styles, and dreams with just their imagination and a hairbrush.

Couture Creations: The Designers Behind Barbie's Wardrobe

In the bright, vibrant world of fashion, Barbie quickly became an iconic muse. But did you know that some of the world's most famous fashion designers lent their creativity to dress her up? Let's dive into this glittering realm and meet the creative talent who turned fabric and thread into miniature masterpieces for our beloved doll.

Calvin Klein (1996): In 1996, the "Calvin Klein Jeans Barbie" hit the shelves. She captured the essence of the '90s with her modern and minimalistic style – a gray tee, denim jeans skirt, and a varsity jacket donning the iconic Calvin Klein logo, embodying the casual elegance that Klein is known for.

Christian Dior (1997): The year was 1997, and in a magnificent blend of toy and haute couture, Barbie donned the famous "Christian Dior Paris" outfit. Echoing the luxury of Dior's Paris runways, this Barbie was draped in a stunning full skirt and a stylish hat, making this classic Parisian diva one of the most memorable Barbie to date.

Giorgio Armani (2003): Armani's design philosophy of elegance and sophistication was showcased in 2003's "Giorgio Armani Barbie". Draped in a shimmering chiffon gown with a striking long skirt that featured intricate, delicate embroidery, she became the epitome of modern, timeless beauty.

Vera Wang (2008): Known for her breathtaking bridal gowns, Vera Wang turned Barbie into a dream bride in 2008. Dressed in a beautiful strapless tulle gown with a delicately embroidered bodice, "The Romanticist Barbie" looked like she had stepped out of a fairy tale.

These iconic designers didn't just dress Barbie – they told stories. Each outfit, and each accessory, was a reflection of the era's fashion trends and the designer's unique style.

So, the next time you hold a Barbie, know that you're not just holding a doll. You're holding a piece of fashion history, a canvas where the world's greatest designers painted their dreams. And through these collaborations, Barbie continued to inspire, proving that fashion is not just about clothes. It's an art, a passion, and most of all, a way to dream big!

Did you know?

There are many fashion designers that have lent their signature looks to Barbie over the years. Try to find them all in this Word Search. Words can be horizontal, vertical, or diagonal, forward or backward, and can overlap. There is no space between names, so a name like "Anne Klein" becomes "anneklein". Turn the page for the solution.

```
L  E  N  B  Y  E  J  Y  O  L  I  W  F  S  X
W  A  A  R  X  H  O  G  N  I  M  U  Y  N  W
B  R  N  E  K  I  C  Z  Q  O  B  E  P  I  O
I  E  N  C  I  V  A  N  J  K  S  J  H  C  H
L  R  E  N  R  W  K  D  E  C  Y  E  A  O  N
L  R  K  E  A  I  C  D  A  V  Z  W  N  L  O
Y  E  L  P  L  T  L  D  P  K  I  U  A  E  L
B  H  E  S  P  A  A  S  N  V  Y  G  E  M  A
O  Q  I  L  H  W  Z  C  W  E  G  M  M  I  M
Y  B  N  O  L  C  U  D  H  R  F  K  O  L  I
Z  G  O  R  A  W  D  O  G  S  L  T  R  L  L
P  Z  N  A  U  B  O  B  M  A  C  K  I  E  L
J  D  Y  C  R  U  T  B  Z  C  F  X  E  R  E
J  D  U  N  E  Q  C  A  G  E  O  G  K  X  R
L  N  Q  T  N  B  U  R  B  E  R  R  Y  K  D
```

- ☐ Anne Klein
- ☐ Billy Boy
- ☐ Bob Mackie
- ☐ Burberry
- ☐ Carol Spencer
- ☐ Escada
- ☐ Givenchy
- ☐ Herrera
- ☐ Hanae Mori
- ☐ Nicole Miller
- ☐ Nolan Miller
- ☐ Ralph Lauren
- ☐ Versace
- ☐ Yuming

Solution

```
L  E  N  B  Y  E  J  Y  O  L  I  W  F  S  X
W  A  A  R  X  H  O  G  N  I  M  U  Y  N  W
B  R  N  E  K  I  C  Z  Q  O  B  E  P  I  O
I  E  N  C  I  V  A  N  J  K  S  J  H  C  H
L  R  E  N  R  W  K  D  E  C  Y  E  A  O  N
L  R  K  E  A  I  C  D  A  V  Z  W  N  L  O
Y  E  L  P  L  T  L  D  P  K  I  U  A  E  L
B  H  E  S  P  A  A  S  N  V  Y  G  E  M  A
O  Q  I  L  H  W  Z  C  W  E  G  M  M  I  M
Y  B  N  O  L  C  U  D  H  R  F  K  O  L  I
Z  G  O  R  A  W  D  O  G  S  L  T  R  L  L
P  Z  N  A  U  B  O  B  M  A  C  K  I  E  L
J  D  Y  C  R  U  T  B  Z  C  F  X  E  R  E
J  D  U  N  E  Q  C  A  G  E  O  G  K  X  R
L  N  Q  T  N  B  U  R  B  E  R  R  Y  K  D
```

- ☐ AnneKlein
- ☐ BillyBoy
- ☐ BobMackie
- ☐ Burberry
- ☐ CarolSpencer
- ☐ Escada
- ☐ Givenchy
- ☐ Herrera
- ☐ HanaeMori
- ☐ NicoleMiller
- ☐ NolanMiller
- ☐ RalphLauren
- ☐ Versace
- ☐ Yuming

Chapter 6
Barbie's World

"The best way to make a friend
is to be a friend."
— Barbie: Mariposa, 2008

I n the pastel-colored rooms of many children in the 1960s, one could often hear the chatters and giggles of imagination taking flight. While Barbie was a shining star, she wasn't alone in her sparkling universe. A tapestry of friends, each with their distinct personalities and backstories, joined her, making playtime a delightful ensemble of stories, adventures, and dreams.

Enter Ken

The year was 1961, and on a sunny day in the fictional Willows, Wisconsin, Barbie's world welcomed Ken Carson. With his sharp crew cut and an ever-so-charming smile, Ken was not just Barbie's boyfriend but her partner in countless adventures. Named after the Handlers' son, he came with his own line of outfits, ranging from casual beachwear to dapper tuxedos. Over the years, Ken evolved, reflecting the changing times and fashion. But through all those transformations, his role remained: to be by Barbie's side, supporting her endeavors and dreams.

Midge Hadley Joins the Scene

1963 brought with it a whirlwind of red hair and freckles in the form of Midge Hadley, Barbie's best friend. With her playful spirit and ever-ready attitude for a new escapade, Midge was every bit the girl next door. Unlike Barbie, who had an extensive career list, Midge was more focused on friendships, relationships, and the everyday adventures of life. She served as a wonderful reflection of the joy of simple pleasures.

Little Skipper

1964 was a special year for Barbie. It was the year she became a big sister. Skipper, with her youthful exuberance, brought a different kind of joy to Barbie's world. She was not just a doll; she was a symbol of the bond of sisterhood. With her shorter stature and teen-like features, Skipper was relatable to younger fans of Barbie. She represented the bridge between childhood innocence and the coming-of-age aspirations that her older sister Barbie portrayed.

Christie

In the lively cityscape of the Barbie universe, 1968 marked a significant year with the introduction of Christie, a radiant African-American doll with a heart full of dreams and adventures and an impecable sense of fashion.

Christie and Barbie shared an instant bond, their friendship transcending the boundaries of the toy box. Together, they embarked on countless escapades, from sun-soaked beach vacations to glamorous parties in the heart of the city. But it wasn't just their shared love for adventure that made them inseparable; it was their mutual respect and understanding of each other's backgrounds and stories. Christie's arrival was more than just a new doll on the shelves; she was a symbol of a changing world, an affirmation for young girls everywhere that beauty, ambition, and friendship come in many forms.

Kira/ Miko

As the sun set in the 1980s and rose into the 1990s, the Barbie universe expanded yet again, introducing an energetic and vibrant character named Miko, later known as Kira. Hailing from Asia, with her long raven-black hair and expressive eyes, Miko brought a touch of the East to Barbie's world, merging traditions with the pulse of contemporary life. Their friendship was instant, a blend of mutual admiration and shared zest for adventure.

Miko, with her rich cultural background, introduced Barbie and their friends to new experiences, from traditional dances to festive celebrations. And in turn, Barbie showed Miko the thrills of Malibu beach parties and star-studded premieres. Kira's presence illuminated the message that friendship, dreams, and aspirations know no borders, and every girl, regardless of where she's from, has a unique story to tell.

Together, this entourage expanded Barbie's universe. They introduced themes of relationships, friendships, family, and the simple joys of everyday life. Barbie's world was no longer just about her; it was about a community, a family, and the myriad of stories and adventures they could have together. In doing so, Mattel gave every child the tools to craft intricate tales of their own, mirroring life's many facets.

Barbie wasn't just a doll; she was a lifestyle. As years rolled by, the enchanting world of Barbie grew beyond her wardrobe, introducing a fascinating array of homes, vehicles, and pets. Each addition was not merely a toy, but a canvas for limitless imagination, giving children the tools to craft stories, adventures, and dreams.

Barbie's first Dream House was introduced in 1962. Made of cardboard with a pink and white design, it was a reflection of the mid-century modern architecture of the time. As the years progressed, so did the grandeur of her homes. There was the Townhouse with an elevator, the Dream Cottage complete with a white picket fence, and the sprawling Magic Mansion with voice-activated lights.

Each home came furnished with intricate details, from velvet couches to tiny bookshelves stocked with mini books, allowing kids to set the stage for Barbie's life, whether she was hosting a party, having a quiet evening by the fireplace, or simply lounging by the pool.

Barbie's adventures weren't limited to her home. In 1962, Barbie got her first car - a chic Austin-Healey roadster in shades of turquoise and rose. Later, she cruised in style with the Barbie Glam Convertible, the iconic pink Corvette, and even an ultra-modern Camper Van for road trips and camping escapades. Each vehicle was a statement of freedom, empowerment, and style, allowing kids to take Barbie and her friends on countless road trips, beach outings, and cross-country adventures.

And as she took center stage in countless adventures, life was never lonely for Barbie. It wasn't just Ken, Midge, or Skipper keeping her company. Barbie had a heart for animals. Over the years, she adopted numerous pets, starting with a horse named Dancer in 1961. Then came cats, dogs, and even exotic animals like a panda and a zebra. Perhaps the most iconic of her pets was Tawny, the horse, and Blaire, her cuddly Golden Retriever. These pets added layers of play, from teaching the responsibility of caring for a pet to adventurous tales of Barbie riding with the wind on her horse.

Each accessory, whether it was a dream house, a sleek car, or a furry friend, was a chapter in the storybook of Barbie's world. They were tools of imagination, allowing children to craft tales of adventure, dreams, friendship, and everyday life. Through these, Barbie's world transformed from a mere plaything to a mirror reflecting the myriad possibilities of life.

Did you know?

Barbie loves animals, and over the years she has adopted many dogs, cats and horses. She was playing with these lovely puppies the other day, but there was a problem with the photo. Can you spot the 7 errors? Turn the page for the solution.

Chapter 7
Infinitely Talented Barbie

"Magic happens when you believe in yourself."

— Barbie: A Fashion Fairytale, 2010

Barbie was never just a pretty face in a world of glitz and glamour. Her journey throughout the years has been one of ambition, inspiration, and versatility. It was essential for Barbie, an icon for countless girls, to not only reflect the changing times but also to inspire and reaffirm that girls could be anything they dreamed of.

Every time Barbie donned a new professional outfit—whether it was the uniform of an astronaut, the white coat of a doctor, or the robes of a judge—it was a statement: *"You can do this too."*

Children everywhere reacted with excitement and wonder. With each new career Barbie adopted, playtimes transformed into ambitious storytelling sessions. Bedrooms became courtrooms, living rooms turned into news stations, and backyards morphed into archaeological dig sites. Barbie wasn't just a doll; she became a vessel for young girls to see themselves in roles they once thought were out of reach.

Barbie's diverse careers played an integral role in shaping young minds. She presented a world where gender barriers were broken, and dreams weren't limited by societal expectations. For many, Barbie was more than a toy; she was a beacon of possibility. Through her, young girls across the globe were reminded that their aspirations were valid, important, and attainable. Barbie's careers were not just about play; they were about empowerment, inspiration, and the promise of a future where girls could, and would, shine brightly in any field they chose.

Barbie's Many Careers

Actress	Dentist	Architect
Camerawoman	Doctor	Chemist
Dancer	Nurse	Computer engineer
Film director	Pediatrician	Entomologist
Musician	Surgeon	Game developer
Photographer	Veterinarian	Marine biologist
		Robotics engineer
		Paleontologist
Baseball player	Firefighter	Scientist
Boxer	Lifeguard	
Gymnast	Mountie	Army medic
Skateboarder	Paramedic	Air force pilot
Skier	Park ranger	Judge
Surfer	Police officer	Teacher
Tennis Player		UNICEF Ambassador
		US President

Barbie's First Careers

With Barbie's keen sense for fashion, it's no surprise that her first gig was as a Fashion Designer, in 1960. With her portfolio at hand and a striking business suit, Barbie was ready to take the world by storm. But she wasn't content to stay in the fashion world. The very next year Barbie took to the skies as a flight attendant, mirroring the glamor and excitement associated with air travel during the 1960s. This was a career that young girls at the time dreamt of, with its promise of adventures and a unique opportunity to see the world.

1961 was a big year for Barbie and for the young girls worldwide that had fallen under her spell. Barbie became a nurse, venturing into the medical field with charm and competence. She was also a Ballerina, and the very next year Barbie took to the tennis courts against Ken.

Always the brainiac, a professional Barbie with a grown-up short bob became a college graduate in 1963. Inspired by no other than the First Lady Jackie Kennedy, Barbie also dawned the iconic 60s pillow hat and business suit, ready for anything life had to throw at her.

But Barbie's most iconic career was just around the corner, as she embraced the space race and became an Astronaut in 1965. Barbie the Astronaut was an immense hit, as she became the first female American to "take to the sky" decades before Sally Rider would make that dream a reality in 1983.

And that was the secret to Barbie's success. While a generation of pioneer career women were breaking glass ceilings and struggling to get a foothold in a wide range of male-dominated fields, Barbie was there alongside them. She normalized the presence of women in professions varying from medicine, to science, to sports, to air force pilots. And all the while she kept on pursuing the feminine interests that launched her in the first place, always with a keen eye for fashion, dancing, and singing.

It seemed that there was nothing that Barbie couldn't do. And young girls worldwide were there right alongside her. For these girls, Barbie the surgeon or Barbie the Navy Officer was just as normal as Barbie the dancer. They were daydreaming about careers that their mothers would never have contemplated, and many of them grew up to become just that — strong, empowered women that were confident to step into any role.

The reception to these career-focused Barbies was overwhelmingly positive. Parents appreciated the message of ambition and possibility Barbie represented, while kids loved the storytelling potential each new profession brought. Discussions arose around dinner tables, with young girls voicing their aspirations to fly to the moon or heal the sick, inspired by their favorite doll.

These early career choices set the stage for a legacy of diversity and ambition in Barbie's world. They signaled that Barbie wasn't just about fashion and beauty; she was about dreams, achievements, and breaking barriers. Each new career was a step towards a world where girls could see themselves as leaders, adventurers, and innovators.

Did you know?

There truly seems to be no job too big or too small for Barbie! With her positive attitude, she's always willing to learn new things and give it all a try. What about you? What are your dream careers?

You're still young and it's perfectly normal not to be sure yet and to change your mind. Even grown-ups are always changing careers and trying something new. The important thing is to try, and never sell yourself short. As Barbie always says,

"You can do anything."

Step One

1. What career are you interested in? If you don't know the exact name, describe it. _____

2. Go online and search for the career. Summarize the main tasks/responsibilities in bullet points:

_____

_____

_____

3. What kind of skills do you need for this career?

_____

_____

_____

4. Are there companies or institutions near where you live that employ in this area? Make a list:

_____

_____

_____

Great job! Now that you know more about your dream career, it's time to talk to someone who actually works in the field. This can be a family friend or maybe even someone who works at one of these companies you listed.

It's extremely important that you keep your parents or guardian involved in this step and in your conversation with any adults, whether you're talking online or in person. A well-intentioned mentor will not want to keep your conversation a secret, and if anyone tells you to "keep it between us" that's an immediate red flag that something is wrong.

If you arrange to meet your mentor, always do so in the company of your parent or guardian. Always meet in a public space and during work hours. Never meet with adults alone and without informing your parents — even if that person is a friend of the family! Remember to be polite, take notes, and always thank the person for their time.

Step Two

It's time to talk to someone who actually works in your dream career. There's nothing like asking questions to a real-person, and who knows, maybe that person might become a long-term mentor to help you in your journey. Here are some suggestions for questions:

1. Can you describe a typical day in your job?

2. What part of your work do you find the most interesting/ challenging?

3. What are the most important skills for your job?

4. How did you get started?

5. What advice would you give to someone who wants to get started in your line of work?

6. What education or training do you recommend?

7. Are there things I could start doing today to help me prepare for a career in this field?

8. Does your company offer internships or summer jobs that I might be able to take in a few years?

Now that you know more about your future career, it's time to make plans. It's never too early — or too late — to learn new skills and try something new. Even if you're still very young, there are ways in which you can try your dream career and see if it really suits you. For this step, you might benefit from the help of your best friend, an older sibling, your parents or a school conselor. And remember to have fun.

You've got this!

1. What new thing did you find out about your dream career?

2. What can you do today to start preparing?

3. What are the skills you'll need? How can you start learning them?

4. Are there related activities such as after-school programs or summer camps near where you live that you can join?

5. Are there companies where you can do internships or volunteer work in an area related to that of your dream career?

Chapter 8
Barbie in Pop Culture

"It feels good to be part of something bigger than yourself"

- Barbie in A Mermaid Tale 2, 2012

From the moment Barbie stepped onto the scene in 1959, she wasn't just a doll. She became an icon, a reflection of the times, and a muse that captivated the imagination of people around the world. Over the decades, Barbie's impact has transcended the toy aisles, embedding herself into the very fabric of global pop culture.

There are few for whom the name "Barbie" does not immediately recall clear childhood images, and of course, the iconic, always smiling, blond-haired girl.

Music and Barbie

Music artists have often referenced Barbie in their lyrics, reinforcing her status as a cultural icon. One of the most notable mentions was in Aqua's 1997 hit "Barbie Girl," a catchy tune that played on Barbie's glamorous lifestyle. But it wasn't just a one-off. Over the years, Barbie has been referenced in numerous songs spanning various genres, highlighting her universal appeal.

Film and Television

Barbie's presence in film and television is undeniable. From starring in her own direct-to-video animated films like "Barbie in the Nutcracker" to appearing in popular TV series, her influence has only grown. She's even had cameo appearances in blockbuster movies such as "Toy Story," further emphasizing her entrenched position in pop culture.

The 2023 "Barbie" film brought the beloved doll back to the big screens, this time with a whimsical mix of live-action actors and a fantasy doll world. The film captures Barbie's self-discovery journey as she battles questions of identity and finding her place in the world, much like the real Barbie doll. The film was staggeringly well-received, making it an immediate summer blockbuster.

Memes, Social Media, and Modern Culture

With the rise of the internet and social media, Barbie found new ways to be relevant. She's been meme-fied, turned into GIFs, and has even had viral moments on platforms like TikTok and Instagram. Mattel's official Barbie Style Instagram account, showcasing Barbie's outfits and lifestyle, has garnered a significant following, proving her timeless appeal.

Art and Exhibitions

Artists, too, have taken Barbie as a muse, often using her to comment on societal norms, beauty standards, and the changing times. From photography series to sculptures, Barbie has been reinterpreted in countless ways.

In 1986, the legendary artist Andy Warhol immortalized Barbie in one of his signature pop art pieces. Warhol's "Barbie" painting captured the essence of the doll as a cultural symbol, bridging the gap between childhood nostalgia and commentary on mass consumerism.

Museums have also recognized Barbie's significance. Exhibitions have been dedicated to charting her evolution, from her 1959 debut to her contemporary iterations. These exhibitions typically showcase rare dolls, original sketches, and prototypes, offering an insightful journey into Barbie's world and the societal shifts she has mirrored.

Celebrity Barbies

In the ever-expanding universe of Barbie, some of the most unique and sought-after dolls are those inspired by real-life celebrities. Throughout the years, Mattel has collaborated with numerous iconic figures, capturing their likenesses, signature styles, and in some cases, even their personalities in doll form. These dolls not only embody the essence of these stars but also reflect the styles, tastes, and pop culture moments that defined their peak years.

Elvis Presley & Priscilla (2000s): Taking a nostalgic trip back to the '60s, the Elvis and Priscilla Barbie set was released in the new millennium. Dressed in their wedding finery, they're a timeless tribute to rock 'n' roll royalty.

Beyoncé (2005): Mattel honored the "Single Ladies" singer by immortalizing her in doll form, highlighting her look from the film "Dreamgirls" — a nod to both her musical and cinematic achievements.

Jennifer Lopez (2013): A dual tribute to her roles as a chart-topping singer and a Hollywood actress, the Jennifer Lopez Barbie showcased the diva's diverse talents and trademark style.

Zendaya (2015): A contemporary icon, the Zendaya Barbie was released to commemorate her stylish appearance at a red-carpet event, complete with her dreadlocks, making a powerful statement.

Ava DuVernay (2015): As part of the "Sheroes" series, the director of critically acclaimed films like "Selma" was honored with a Barbie doll. She was depicted with her signature dreadlocks and a director's chair, encapsulating her visionary spirit.

BTS (2019): Catering to the global K-Pop phenomenon, each of the seven members of BTS, the world's biggest boy band, were crafted into their own individual Barbie dolls, embodying the spirit of the contemporary music scene.

J.K. Rowling (2019): Honoring the literary genius behind the Harry Potter series, Mattel released a J.K. Rowling Barbie. Dressed in a smart ensemble, the doll captured the elegance and intellect of the renowned author, wielding a quill and manuscript, symbolizing her immense contribution to literature.

Billie Jean King (2020): A symbol of strength, activism, and unparalleled skill in tennis, Billie Jean King's Barbie came donned in her classic tennis attire, celebrating her sportsmanship and advocacy for gender equality.

Did you know?

There are many celebrities that have been immortalized as Barbies and Kens over the years. Can you guess who these celebrity "Kens"are? There are no spaces between names, so write NameSurname. Turn the page for the solution.

Across
3. British musician known for "Rocket Man" and "Candle in the Wind."
5. American singer who gained fame as the runner-up on "American Idol" and later fronted the band Queen since 2011.
6. Renowned singer known as "Ol' Blue Eyes" and "The Voice."

Down
1. Versatile actor who portrayed Captain Jack Sparrow in the "Pirates of the Caribbean" film series.
2. Legendary rock artist with different color eyes and hits like "Space Oddity" and "Ziggy Stardust."
4. Country music superstar known for hits like "Live Like You Were Dying" and "Humble and Kind."

What about these celebrity "Barbies", can you guess who they are? There are no spaces between names, so write NameSurname. Solution on the next page.

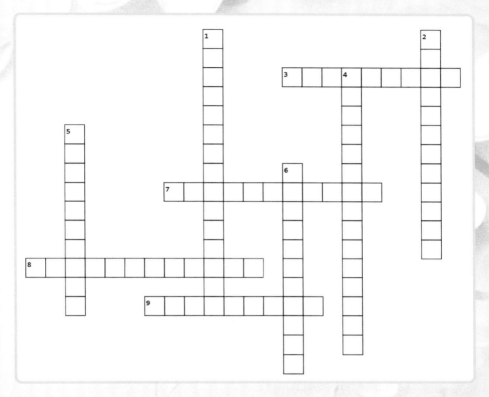

Across
3. Pop superstar known for hits like "Firework," "Roar," and "I Kissed a Girl."
7. Pop singer with the hits "Girls Just Want to Have Fun" and "Time After Time."
8. Pop icon and multi-talented performer, known for hits like "Nasty," "Rhythm Nation," and "Together Again."
9. Motown legend and lead singer of The Supremes, known for her successful solo career and hits like "Ain't No Mountain High Enough" and "I'm Coming Out."

Down
1. Emmy-winning actress who portrayed Dana Scully in "The X-Files" and later starred as Jean Milburn in "Sex Education."
2. Actress who played Princess Leia in the original "Star Wars" franchise.
4. Hollywood legend and two-time Oscar-winning actress, known for her roles in "Cleopatra" and "Who's Afraid of Virginia Woolf?"
5. The "Queen of Rock 'n' Roll," an iconic singer known for hits like "What's Love Got to Do with It" and "Proud Mary."
6. Oscar-winning actress who portrayed Rose in "Titanic" and won acclaim for her role in "The Reader."

Solutions

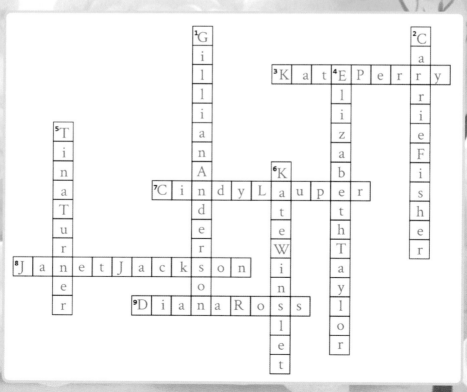

Chapter 9
Barbie's Evolution

"Even the smallest person
can make a big difference."
- Barbie Presents Thumbelina, 2009

I n a world ever-evolving, Barbie wasn't just a doll on a shelf; she was a reflection of society's shifts, changes, and aspirations. As the world around her transformed, so did she, always adapting and growing, ensuring she remained relevant and representative of the times.

The Swingin' Sixties: The 1960s saw Barbie capturing the spirit of the decade. As the women's liberation movement took hold and cultural revolutions spread, Barbie's world too started to reflect a broader range of possibilities. It was during this decade that she first ventured into the professional world, showing that Barbie and young girls were more than just pretty faces.

The Groovy Seventies: The 1970s brought about changes in fashion and societal values, and Barbie was right there, echoing the era's sentiments. With the rise of the feminist movement, Barbie embraced more empowered roles. This was the period when "Malibu Barbie" made her debut, showcasing a more laid-back, sun-kissed California vibe.

Donning a chic turquoise bathing suit, trendy sunglasses, and a bright yellow towel draped over her arm, Malibu Barbie was the embodiment of the beach-loving spirit. She was the girl who wasn't confined to a house or limited to city life. Instead, she thrived under the open sky, with the Pacific Ocean as her backyard.

But Malibu Barbie wasn't just about aesthetics. She symbolized the free spirit of the decade, embracing the "California Cool" attitude. The ocean was no longer just a place for boys to surf; Barbie, with her beach-ready look, declared the waves were hers to conquer too.

The Bold Eighties: As women began to make significant strides in the corporate world in the 1980s, "Day-to-Night Barbie" was introduced. She was a chic executive by day and a glamorous diva by night. This duality spoke to the era's theme of women managing multifaceted roles with elegance and flair.

The Tech-Savvy Nineties: The 1990s saw a technological revolution, and Barbie wasn't left behind. This was the age of "Computer Engineer Barbie," symbolizing the increasing role of women in STEM fields. With the world entering the digital age, Barbie showcased that girls could be tech-savvy and break barriers in male-dominated sectors.

The 2000s and 2010s: Body Positivity and Beyond: The new millennium brought about another crucial conversation: body image. The "Fashionista" line, introduced in 2016, was a revolutionary step forward. Barbie dolls now came in various body types - tall, petite, and curvy, along with a broader range of skin tones, eye colors, and hairstyles. Barbie started to look more like the everyday woman, not just an unattainable ideal. In 2020, Mattel introduced a Barbie with vitiligo and another without hair, highlighting the beauty in differences and bringing visibility to conditions that were often underrepresented.

Barbie and Beauty Standards

In the heart of many a childhood memory, Barbie has long held her spot as a beacon of glamor, beauty, and aspiration. However, her influence extends far beyond innocent play and into the realms of society's perceptions of beauty, identity, and even self-worth.

From her inception in 1959, Barbie's slender figure, long blonde hair, and blue eyes became emblematic of a Western beauty ideal. With her hourglass figure, long legs, and tiny waist, she was emblematic of the aspirational beauty standards of the late 50s, reflecting the image of stars like Marylin Monroe, Elizabeth Taylor, and Audrey Hepburn.

But in a world where representation plays a vital role in shaping self-perception, Barbie's singular, unattainable inadvertently emphasized a specific beauty archetype, leading many to question and criticize the narrow perspective of attractiveness.

The criticism wasn't solely about her facial features or her blonde locks. Barbie's unrealistic body proportions stirred debates about body image issues among young girls. It was estimated that if translated to human dimensions, her measurements would result in an unlikely and unhealthy physique, further pushing the narrative of an unattainable beauty standard.

As societies evolved, so did their understanding of beauty. With the rise of movements emphasizing body positivity, diversity, and genuine representation in the media, Mattel found itself amidst growing concerns and critiques about Barbie's role in shaping these societal norms.

Recognizing the winds of change and in response to these critiques, the turn of the 21st century saw Mattel undertake a seismic shift in how Barbie was portrayed. The introduction of dolls from diverse

racial backgrounds, varying body types, different abilities, and a broader spectrum of careers was a definitive statement of intent. The "Fashionistas" line in 2016 was revolutionary – it featured tall, petite, and curvy Barbies, breaking the mold of the 'classic' Barbie physique.

Barbies with vitiligo, prosthetic limbs, and bald dolls have entered the scene, signaling a more inclusive understanding of beauty. These changes not only mirror society's evolving standards of beauty but also play a part in driving that very evolution, reinforcing the idea that beauty is not one-size-fits-all.

Yet, the influence of the iconic Barbie doll on shaping and reflecting societal beauty norms cannot be understated. She remains a subject of both admiration and critique, symbolizing the constant dance between media representation and societal expectations. What remains evident is that as society grows in its understanding and acceptance of diverse beauty, Barbie will likely continue to evolve, serving both as a reflection of and an influence on the ever-changing standards of beauty.

Barbie and Diversity

Throughout her journey, Barbie's cultural evolution has been a testament to her enduring appeal. By mirroring the changes, challenges, and celebrations of each decade, she has provided a snapshot of history, always reminding young girls that they too can evolve, grow, and make a difference in the world.

But while Barbie was revolutionary in the 1960s, as the decades passed the doll that once encouraged young girls to dream big started to be attacked by feminists and the public alike. She was after all a pretty, slim, blue-eyed blond girl, reinforcing a beauty stereotype that no longer resonates with a multicultural and diverse world.

Over the decades, Mattel made many attempts to catch up with the times and respond to the public desire for a more diverse and inclusive "Barbie". Some of these attempts have been more successful than others, but they all paved the way for the continuous success and popularity of the brand.

African-American Barbie

As the 1960s unfolded, the Civil Rights Movement was making headlines, challenging long-held societal norms and pushing for equal rights for African Americans. Inside the walls of Mattel, there was an echoing sentiment. Workers on Mattel's production line, many of whom were themselves people of color, had been quietly but persistently advocating for a Black Barbie since the early 1960s. They recognized the significance of representation and the power a toy could have in shaping young minds.

In 1968, Mattel introduced Christie, Barbie's first Black friend. But while her skin was darker, her features were strikingly similar to Barbie's. This was because Christie was made using the same mold as Barbie, resulting in a doll that, while dark-skinned, had distinctly Caucasian features. To many, this was a half-step—recognition of the need for diversity but not a full embrace of it.

The reception to Christie in the African-American community was mixed. On one hand, many were thrilled to see a Black doll in the Barbie lineup. Children could finally play with a doll that looked more like them, and parents appreciated this nod to diversity. However, Caucasian features on a dark-skinned doll felt inauthentic to some, and there was a sense that Mattel was merely adapting to societal pressures rather than genuinely understanding and celebrating Black beauty.

It's worth noting that while Christie was a groundbreaking introduction to the world of Barbie, she wasn't the first Black doll on the market. Other Black dolls had been available since the early 20th century, but many of these were steeped in racial stereotypes. Christie's introduction was part of a broader movement in the toy industry toward more authentic and positive representation.

It wasn't until the late 1970s and early 1980s that Christie received a new facial mold, one that better represented African-American features. This change was a testament to the growing awareness and understanding of the importance of authentic representation, not just in skin color but in features and expression.

Teresa: A New Friend from Across the Border

In the 1980s, as the Barbie universe continued to grow, Mattel recognized the importance of embracing the rich tapestry of cultures that make up America. This was an era where the nation was becoming increasingly aware of its multicultural identity. There was a rising consciousness about the contributions and significance of Latino communities across the U.S.

Enter Teresa in 1988, Barbie's Latina friend, bringing with her a fresh face and a cultural background that had not been previously represented in Barbie's circle. With wavy brown hair, a sun-kissed complexion, and a radiant smile, Teresa was not just a doll, but a symbol of an entire community seeking mainstream representation.

Her introduction was significant, especially for countless Latino children who, for the first time, saw a Barbie friend who shared their heritage. They could imagine stories that felt closer to their own lived experiences, making playtime even more immersive and meaningful.

But, as with any attempt at representation, there were complexities. The Latino community is vast, spanning numerous countries, cultures, and histories. Some felt that Teresa, while a step in the right direction, was still a broad-stroke attempt to encapsulate this diverse community. However, many others appreciated the gesture, recognizing that one doll couldn't possibly represent every nuance of the Latino experience but valuing the visibility she provided.

As years passed, Teresa's character evolved, adapting to the times and reflecting the dynamic nature of the Latino community in the U.S. and globally. Through fashion choices, playsets, and storylines, Mattel made efforts to showcase different aspects of Latino culture, ensuring Teresa was more than just a token character, but rather a vibrant and integral part of Barbie's world.

Embracing Diversity in the New Millennium

The 2000s and 2010s marked significant shifts in Barbie's representation. As discussions about body positivity, inclusivity, and global representation became more mainstream, Mattel responded. As decades passed, the Barbie brand began to embrace that beauty and representation are not one-size-fits-all. The traditional Barbie, with her 50s-inspired hourglass figure, was quickly becoming out of tune with modern times.

With this enlightenment came a wave of new dolls, characterized by a rich tapestry of shapes, sizes, and backgrounds, all echoing the vibrant diversity of the real world. The Fashionistas line, launched in the 2010s, marked a significant shift. Before this, Barbie had primarily held to a specific standard of beauty: tall, slender, and predominantly white. However, with the introduction of this line, Barbie's world opened up. Dolls with petite, tall, and curvy body types made their appearance, shaking up the traditional mold.

It wasn't just about different body shapes; skin tones ranging from very pale to deep, hair textures from straight to curly to beautifully coiled, and a multitude of ethnic backgrounds were introduced. Even Barbie's feet underwent a transformation, allowing her to switch between heels and flats for the first time.

Diversity wasn't just about looks. Barbie's companion, Ken, who had for years been in a fixed role as her boyfriend, started to see a transformation as well. The "Next Gen Ken" lineup in 2017 introduced diverse Kens – broad, slim, and original. Their hairstyles varied from cornrows to man buns, representing the diverse ways modern men express themselves. Ken's evolution wasn't just skin deep; it reflected a societal shift away from rigid gender norms and roles, signaling that boys and men could be just as diverse, fashionable, and expressive as girls and women.

Mattel's efforts extended beyond body and gender representation. They introduced dolls like Barbie's friend Becky, who uses a wheelchair, and later versions of the doll were designed with more accurate accessibility features. Another shining moment in Barbie's journey toward inclusivity was the introduction of a Barbie with a prosthetic limb and another with the skin condition vitiligo.

These strides were not without challenges. While many praised Mattel for their efforts, critics pointed out occasional missteps or oversight in representation. Yet, through both acclaim and criticism, one thing became clear: Barbie's world was no longer a monolithic representation of beauty and identity. It had transformed into a mosaic, ever-evolving, striving to mirror the complexities and beauty of the real world.

In an ever-changing world, Barbie remains not just a mirror, but an active voice championing societal progression and inclusivity. With each decade, Mattel pushes Barbie's boundaries, ensuring she continues to be an empowering figure, relevant to the present time.

Long before formal representation, various editions of Barbie, due to their flamboyant outfits and unique styles, were embraced by parts of the LGBTQ+ community. They became icons, signaling freedom of expression and breaking away from societal norms. However, it wasn't until more recent years that Mattel began consciously designing dolls that spoke directly to the community.

In 2019, Mattel launched a set of Proudly Pink Barbie dolls, causing a stir with their vibrant, LGBTQ+-inspired colors. The line was an affirmation and celebration of the community, with many interpreting it as a nod to the Transgender Pride Flag colors. Later, in a collaboration with fashion brand Moschino, a doll set featuring Barbie and Ken was released, where Ken donned a "Moschino" T-shirt styled after the one worn by Moschino's openly gay creative director, Jeremy Scott. The set was seen as a celebration of LGBTQ+ fashion influence and creativity.

Recently, Barbie also began to touch on delicate topics like mental health. Recognizing the immense pressure young kids face in today's digitized, high-expectation society, Mattel sought to provide tools for children to articulate and understand their feelings. New editions of Barbie dolls came equipped with calming tools, like breathing exercises and journaling kits. They served a dual purpose: to offer playtime activities while subtly introducing children to mindfulness practices. A range of dolls depicting everyday moments, like a 'Breathe with Me Barbie', was a reminder that it's okay to pause and take a moment for oneself.

The latest step into normalization and acceptance of diversity is the release of the first Barbie doll with Down Syndrome, designed with the support of the National Down Syndrome Society (NDSS).

As Barbie moves into the future, her journey encapsulates more than just the changing fashion or career trends; it reflects an ongoing commitment to showcasing diversity, encouraging inclusivity, and being a beacon of empowerment for all. Mattel's vision for Barbie is clear: a doll that resonates with every child, regardless of their background or challenges, reminding them that they are seen, heard, and celebrated.

Did you know?

Having friends from different backgrounds can be a lot of fun, but it can also be a bit confusing. Things you might take for granted may not be as common for your friends, and sometimes it can be a bit embarrassing to ask.

That's where books and documentaries can be of great help to get to know more about each other's culture. They can help make your relationship stronger and give you more common ground. Here are some suggestions to get you started:

African American

* "Brown Girl Dreaming," by Jacqueline Woodson
* "Piecing Me Together," by Renée Watson
* "Who Put This Song On?" by Morgan Parker

Latinx

* "The Distance Between Us," by Reyna Grande
* "When I Was Puerto Rican," by Esmeralda Santiago
* "The Education of Margot Sánchez," by Lilliam Rivera

East Asia

* "This Place is Still Beautiful," by XiXi Tian
* "Messy Roots: A Graphic Memoir of a Wuhanese American," by Laura Gao
* "The Great Wall of Lucy Wu," by Wendy Wan-Long Shang

Muslim

* "I Am Malala," by Malala Yousafzai andPatricia McCormick
* "Proud: Living My American Dream," by Ibtihaj Muhammad
* "Only This Beautiful Moment," by Abdi Nazemian

LGBTQ+

* "This is Our Rainbow: 16 Stories of Her, Him, Them, and Us," by Katherine Locke and Nicole Melleby (editors)
* "The Lesbiana's Guide to Catholic School," by Sonora Reyes
* "Hani and Ishu's Guide to Fake Dating," by Adiba Jaigirdar
* "Obie is Man Enough," by Schuyler Bailar

Chapter 10
Barbie's Legacy

"Best friends, today, tomorrow, and always."
-- Barbie and The Diamond Castle, 2008

At first glance, a Barbie doll might seem like just another toy on the shelf. Yet, for generations of children, she has represented so much more than that. Dive deep into the world of a child, and you'll uncover the magical allure that makes Barbie not just any other doll, but a cherished friend, a confidante, and a canvas for countless dreams.

Why kids love Barbie

Imagine being in your room, surrounded by toys, and there, standing out among them all, is Barbie. With her by your side, your room is no longer just four walls; it's a spaceship, a deep-sea adventure, a bustling city, or a magical forest. Each day with Barbie is a brand-new story, filled with excitement and imagination.

And Barbie isn't alone in her adventures. She has a group of diverse friends, each with their own stories and backgrounds. Through their tales, you realize that friendship isn't bound by where someone comes from or what they look like. True friends stick together, through thick and thin, just like you and Barbie.

Have you ever had one of those days? Maybe school was tough or things didn't go as planned. On days like those, Barbie is there, sitting on your shelf, ready to listen, ready to be there for you. She's more than just plastic and paint; she's a friend, always there with a comforting smile.

With Barbie, every day is a reminder that you can be anything you want to be. Whether you dream of flying to the moon, diving deep into the ocean, or designing the latest fashion, Barbie shows you that with hard work and imagination, your dreams are within reach.

But beyond the fantastical tales and make-believe scenarios, Barbie instilled deeper lessons. Through her, children learned about empathy, resilience, and determination. They understood that a woman can be anything she wants to be — a president, a scientist, a CEO, an athelte, a designer, as well as a mom and best friend. And that gender is no boundary to ambition.

Many a time, children would whisper their most profound dreams into Barbie's ear, believing that she had the power to make them come true. And in a way, she did. She bolstered their confidence, telling them that they too, like Barbie, could traverse any path they chose.

As years passed and children grew up, the toys they played with often changed. Robots, video games, and gadgets took center stage. But the memories associated with Barbie remained, etched into the canvas of their minds. The dreams she inspired, the stories she helped weave, and the confidence she instilled became integral to their identities.

In shaping dreams and fanning the flames of imagination, Barbie did more than just entertain. She became a cultural icon, a reflection of evolving times, and a steadfast reminder that with belief and imagination, the world truly was one's oyster.

Barbie Goes Green: An Eco-Friendly Adventure

In a world bustling with cars, factories, and bright city lights, Mother Earth started showing signs of weariness. The oceans whispered tales of plastic woes, and the trees sighed with the weight of carbon. Every nook and cranny of the globe echoed the same message: it was time for a change, a shift towards sustainability.

Enter Barbie, the beloved icon of many, with her ever-shiny hair and trendsetting fashion sense. But beyond her glitz and glamor, Barbie had a heart that cared deeply for the planet. As kids worldwide looked up to her, it became essential for Barbie to set an example in this crucial environmental movement.

The brains at Mattel took notice and decided that Barbie needed to adapt and reflect the times' ecological concerns. But how? The first challenge was addressing the plastic issue. Millions of Barbie dolls had been sold worldwide, and if not disposed of properly, they could contribute to the mounting plastic pollution.

In a revolutionary move, Mattel introduced a line of Barbies made from recycled plastics. These dolls, as fabulous as their predecessors, carried a special story: they were crafted from plastic that could have otherwise ended up harming marine life in the oceans. But that wasn't enough. In 2023, Mattel pledged to go plastic-free by 2030, switching production to recyclable materials instead, a bold step in toy manufacturing.

But the eco-initiative didn't stop at the dolls. The packaging, once plastic-laden, was revamped to utilize sustainable materials. It was designed to be recyclable, ensuring that after unboxing their new friend, kids could dispose of the packaging without harming the planet.

Mattel also recognized the importance of education. New Barbie playsets highlighted environmental roles like Marine Biologist and Forest Ranger. Through play, children were subtly introduced to the concept of caring for the planet. The response was heartwarming. Kids embraced the new eco-friendly Barbie, not just as a toy, but as a symbol of change. Parents appreciated the effort to combine play with essential life values, teaching the young generation about sustainability through their favorite doll.

Barbie's transition to a more environmentally conscious figure showed the world that no matter how iconic or established, adapting for the greater good was possible. And in this tale of transformation, Barbie became not just a doll but a beacon of hope for a greener tomorrow.

Digital Barbie

Gone were the days when a child's interaction with Barbie was limited only to the tangible, plastic figure. The dawn of the 21st century saw Barbie venturing into the vibrant world of video games, apps, and even virtual reality.

First came video games. Platforms like Nintendo and PlayStation featured Barbie-themed games where players could embark on thrilling adventures, solve mysteries, or even design fabulous fashion shows. Whether it was horseback riding or exploring enchanted worlds, virtual Barbie became a gamer's best companion.

But the innovation didn't stop there. Recognizing the growing importance of smartphones and tablets, Mattel introduced a series of Barbie apps. These apps allowed kids to design Barbie's outfits, style her hair, and even take her on globetrotting journeys. And just like that, Barbie was right in the pocket, accessible anytime, anywhere!

One of the groundbreaking additions to Barbie's digital universe was the virtual reality (VR) experience. Imagine putting on a VR headset and suddenly finding yourself in Barbie's Dreamhouse, meeting her friends, and going on interactive adventures. It was like diving into a dream, only to realize it was as real as it could get!

These digital innovations not only introduced Barbie to a new generation but also enriched the ways kids could engage with her. It fostered creativity (think digital design studios where you could craft Barbie's next trendy dress) and problem-solving (puzzles, mysteries, and challenges in video games).

But amidst all the pixels and tech, the essence of Barbie remained unchanged. Whether in the physical world or the digital realm, she continued to inspire, entertain, and spark the imagination. As technology continues to evolve, who knows where Barbie might pop up next? The possibilities are as endless as Barbie's timeless charm.

Fun Facts About Barbie

Barbie's world, as glittering and expansive as it is, hides some surprising nuggets of information that many might not know. So, dear readers, let's embark on a whirlwind journey to discover some lesser-known facts about our beloved fashion doll!

Barbie's Full Name: Everyone knows her as Barbie, but did you know her full name is Barbara Millicent Roberts? Quite a regal name for the queen of the doll world!

Barbie's Hometown Vibes: Barbie is often seen with a cosmopolitan flair, but she originally hails from a fictional place called Willows, Wisconsin. That's right; she's a small-town girl at heart.

A Woman of Many Careers: While Barbie's roles as a fashion icon, doctor, and astronaut are widely known, few might be aware that she has had over 200 careers since her inception. She's been a UNICEF ambassador, a presidential candidate, a game developer. You name it, Barbie has tried her hand at it with her usual talent and charm.

Pet Paradise: Barbie loves animals, and not just cats and dogs. Over the years, she's had a zebra, a lion cub, a giraffe, and even a panda.

Barbie's Many Pairs of Shoes: If you've ever wondered how many pairs of shoes Barbie has, the answer might surprise you. Barbie has amassed an astonishing collection of more than one billion pairs of shoes since her debut. Talk about shoe goals!

The Mystery of Her Eyes: For over two decades since her debut, Barbie dolls looked to the side. It wasn't until 1971 that Barbie got a new look, where she stared straight ahead for the first time.

Barbie's Teeny-Tiny World: Ever noticed the ultra-miniature books, pencils, and food items that come with some Barbie sets? In the 1960s, Mattel released a Barbie Dream Store Fashion Department that came with a teeny-tiny tabbed fashion booklet.

The Sound of Music: Barbie isn't just about fashion and careers. In the 80s, she formed a band with her friends called 'Barbie and the Rockers.'

Hidden Talents: Barbie has been a sign language teacher. In the 90s, "Sign Language Barbie" was released, complete with a book on how to sign, encouraging kids to learn and communicate in diverse ways.

First Woman on the Moon? Barbie might not be a real astronaut, but she made it to the moon before Neil Armstrong. In 1965, four years before the first moon landing, "Miss Astronaut Barbie" was released.

Barbie's BFFs: Barbie isn't an only child. She has a little sister named Skipper, and her best friends include Midge, Teresa, and Nikki. She's also got a range of friends from diverse backgrounds, showcasing friendship without borders.

A Silent Film Star: Barbie has appeared in many movies, but did you know she starred in a silent film? In 1997, Barbie starred in a ten-minute, silent short film, "The Adventures of Barbie and G.I. Joe," which played at the Sundance Film Festival.

Fashion Forward: Barbie has always been a fashion icon. Since her creation, Barbie has worn outfits designed by more than seventy famous fashion designers, including Christian Dior, Versace, and Gucci.

The Famous Ponytail: Barbie's iconic ponytail hairstyle was inspired by a popular 1950s hairstyle called a "poodle cut."

Barbie's Luxurious Dreamhouse: Barbie's Dreamhouse has evolved over the years. The latest iteration is a three-story, seven-room townhouse that includes a working elevator.

A Barbie Sold Every Second: Barbie's popularity is nothing short of astounding. On average, a Barbie doll is sold every three seconds somewhere in the world!

With so many hidden surprises in Barbie's world, it makes one wonder: what will she think of next? As decades roll on, Barbie continues to amaze and inspire with her ever-evolving universe.

Books for Kids: Big Ideas for Bright Minds

If you enjoyed this book, why not follow it with another title from our series *"Books for Kids: Big Ideas for Bright Minds."* Each title focuses on an interesting topic for curious young minds, answering the important questions of *why?* and *how?* Whether you want to know what exactly happened to dinosaurs or how fire-fighting evolved through the ages, there's a book here for you.

Why Choose This Series?

Catered for Bright Minds: Each title is intricately crafted to satisfy the insatiable inquisitiveness of young minds. Dive deep into the whys and hows, and come out enlightened.

Vivid Illustrations: Lose yourself in vivid and captivating illustrations that bring every page to vibrant life.

Diverse Topics: With a wide range of subjects, there's always something new and exciting for every curious mind.

Learn the Fun Way: Engaging pedagogical activities ensure that you not only treasure the journey but remember the lessons, too.

Gift your child the gateway to a universe of knowledge, exploration, and wonder. For the brains that never stop questioning, the *"Books for Kids: Big Ideas for Bright Minds"* series is your ultimate answer. Available on paperback and kindle.

Embark on a journey of discovery, one book at a time!

Made in the USA
Middletown, DE
03 November 2023